Alva Bonaker

Between Village and City

Rural-urban linkages in the broader region of Hyderabad

Emerging megacities
Dicussion Papers
Edited by Konrad Hagedorn, Christine Werthmann, Dimitrios Zikos, Ramesh Chennamaneni

Humboldt-Universität zu Berlin
Department of Agricultural Economics
Division of Resource Economics
Philippstr. 13, House 12
10115 Berlin

Tel.: +49 (0)30 2093 6305
Fax: +49 (0)30 2093 6497
www.agrar.hu-berlin.de/struktur/institute/wisola/fg/ress
www.sustainable-hyderabad.de

Contact: emerging.megacities@hu-berlin.de

The emerging megacities discussion papers are available at:
www.eh-verlag.de

ISSN print edition 2193-6927

Emerging megacities Discussion Papers are prepared by researchers working on topics in the realm of sustainable development in Megacities of Tomorrow, a research priority by the German Ministry of Education and Research (BMBF). The papers have been peer-reviewed by a board of external reviewers.
Views and opinions expressed do not necessarily represent those of the Division of Resource Economics.
Comments are highly welcome and should be sent directly to the authors.
We welcome contributions on any topics related to Megacities of Tomorrow. Further information on the submission procedure is given at:
www.sustainable-hyderabad.de/emerging-megacities

Bonaker, Alva

Between Village and City
Rural-urban linkages in the broader region of Hyderabad

Emerging megacities Discussion Papers, Volume 6/2010

ISBN/EAN: 978-3-86741-823-2

First published in 2012 by Europaeischer Hochschulverlag GmbH & Co KG, Bremen, Germany.

© Europaeischer Hochschulverlag GmbH & Co KG, Fahrenheitstr. 1, D-28359 Bremen (www.eh-verlag.de). All rights reserved.

Cover: Photo "Metropolis", ferendus (flickr). Creative Commons License

No part of this publication may be reproduced or transmitted, in any form or by any means, electronic, mechanical, photocopying, recording or otherwise, or stored in any retrieval system of nay nature, without the written permission of the copyright holder and the publisher, application for which shall be made to the publisher.

EHV

Between Village and City
Rural-urban linkages in the broader region of Hyderabad

Alva Bonaker[*]

September 2010

Abstract

The rural-urban linkages in the Hyderabad region are one of the research areas of Work Package 6 "Participation and Communication Strategies" of the project which is dealt with by the nexus Institute for Cooperation Management and Interdisciplinary Research. Nexus examines the quality of rural-urban linkages with the aim to identify the exchange between city and village and establish or strengthen spatial partnerships that can promote energy efficient lifestyles and have a positive effect on social networks. Within this research field the present paper tries to analyse rural-urban migration in this area with focus on changes through new technologies in the city as well as in the villages.

Key words: *rural-urban linkages, migration, rural development, Hyderabad, India*

---

[*] Email: bonaker@nexusinstitut.de, nexus - Institute for Cooperation Management and Interdisciplinary Research GmbH, Otto-Suhr-Allee 59, Berlin

1 Introduction

India as a huge country with an enormous population growth currently faces the situation that the economical and technical domains are internationally recognised for their rapid progress while at the same time large parts of the society are still struggling with poverty and deficient living conditions. This development is very well reflected in the numerous huge metropolises of the country. The South Indian city of Hyderabad (the state capital of Andhra Pradesh), for example, is steadily approaching a population number of ten million. In 2008 the population of the metropolitan area was 7.8 million. The administration of the *Hyderabad Metropolitan Development Authority* (HMDA) covers an area of 6,856 square km being the second largest metropolitan area of the country after Delhi (greatandhra.com 2008). As in other cities, problems of urban planning such as transportation, housing and environmental issues are among the most urgent matters. In order to support the city in coping with these challenges, a project *"Sustainable Hyderabad – Megacity of tomorrow"* (funded by the German Ministry for Education and Research) is run by a range of German as well as Indian institutes and organisations. The overall aim of the project is to develop strategies for improved governance structures and sustainable city development, focusing on low emission lifestyles that allow for better environment protection and enhanced quality of life. Among many other aspects, the rural surroundings of the city play an important role in the context of urban development as both spaces are closely intertwined and connected through urban migration and all kinds of linkages. In cooperation with one of the German partners, nexus (Institute for Cooperation Management and Interdisciplinary Research), this thesis deals with the aspect of rural-urban linkages.

Tracing the question: *How do rural-urban linkages function and which influences do new technologies have on these relations?* The thesis aims to examine the nature and role of rural-urban relations on the example of the broader region of Hyderabad. Starting with a short discussion of rural and urban relations in general, the first chapter suggests that rural and urban spaces interact in complex ways. Hence, to assume a strict dichotomy does not reflect the reality of the people involved. In the following part some aspects of migration, mutual exchange and dependencies between the core of the city and its surroundings are analysed with focus on the situation of people from rural areas. In an attempt to identify changes in rural-urban relations and patterns of migration, the subsequent section focuses on the effects that new developments and technologies in the city or the village have on rural-urban relations. This is especially interesting in Hyderabad since the city is currently experiencing an enormous growth of the information and communication technology (ICT) sector. As it is assumed that this development exclude some parts of society, particularly the rural population, the claim for implementing small projects in rural areas is discussed as well.

While the first part of the paper is based on literature research – mainly on the topics in general but wherever possible with focus on Andhra Pradesh/Hyderabad – in the second part findings from empirical research are at centre of the analysis. Ten expert interviews been have conducted in Hyderabad that cover aspects of rural-urban linkages similar to what has been discussed in the literature sections. Besides the intensity of the linkages and the motivations of people to move from the rural to the urban area and vice versa, requirements for better perspectives for rural areas are examined. Furthermore, a section focusing on new technologies sheds some light on recent changes in rural-urban relations and explores the extent to which technology and linkages to the city can play a role in promoting village development. In the following comparison between findings from the literature and from the interviews, some broad trends are revealed. However, it becomes apparent throughout the analysis that rural-urban linkages are extremely diverse, and that further research is needed.

2 Rural-urban linkages in general

2.1 Rural-urban divide, urban bias and beyond

This section aims to shed some light on the relation and mutual dependencies of rural and urban areas. In earlier literature rural and urban areas were often described as two distinct entities or even as consisting of two separate classes. Lipton (1977) even established his theory of urban bias on the assumption of such kind of strict dichotomy, which he formulates in his often quoted thesis: *The most important conflict in the poor countries of the world today is not between labour and capital. Nor is it between foreign and national interests. It is between the rural classes and the urban classes.* (Ibid: 13). In short, Lipton's concept of the urban bias tries to give an explanation for the phenomenon that development and poverty co-exist. He argues that all the investment goes into things like food, infrastructure, etc. for the urban living instead of basic needs for the rural population. The urban sector, Lipton emphasises, is even successful in buying off the rural elite what further enforces the process of 'urban-biased' allocation and policy. This concept and the underlying assumption of a strict rural-urban divide were challenged by many authors like Ghosh, for example, who emphasises that the concept of the class bias ignores the fact that there are various classes within the urban sector (1991: 12).

In sharp contrast to Lipton many sociologists point out that nowadays the increasing interdependence between the rural and the urban sectors makes a rural-urban dichotomy meaningless. Pocock (1960), for instance, who focuses in his observations on India, points out his strong opposition to a dichotomy between studies concentrating on either urban or rural space in isolation assuming that they are different types of society (even before Lipton established his concept). In a later study, conducted by Lynch about a specific caste of Chamars in Agra, the author finds that Pocock is right in assuming that rural and urban areas are essentially the same (Lynch 1992: 286). Also rejecting Lipton's theory of an urban bias, Shah (1988) argues that with the increasing importance of urban centres, rural-urban relations too play a significant role, which has largely been ignored. He emphasises that there have always been strong linkages between villages and towns or cities against the assumption that the village is a self-sufficient entity, which was long time prevailing in sociological and social anthropological writing. The author points out that beyond kinship relations, which function as a link, there is a vivid exchange between village and city. The village population does not only provide the city with agricultural products but has in turn always taken goods (food, textiles, consumer goods, etc.) and (ritual) services from the city to the village. Another dimension is the diffusion of customs, institutions, ideas, etc. from urban to rural areas by various means of communication, including social links such as those of caste and kinship. However, it took some time until some authors explicitly shifted their focus to studying rural-urban relations and linkages. Steinbrink (2009), for example, analyses informal linkages between city and the countryside. Although his regional focus is Cape Town in South Africa, his study and argumentation of how social networks can be approached and theorised seem to be interesting for international comparison. He points out that even today rural and urban areas (e.g. rural and urban poverty) are generally observed separately and thus the emphasis lies on the dividing aspects instead of seeing the complexity of the picture and the interaction which links the two areas (Ibid: 38, 39). His assumption is that this approach does only lead to symptom reduction but not to a solution for the problems. Thus, he totally rejects to think in terms of localities – city and countryside – but introduces a concept of 'translocal social spheres'. This concept counters the thinking of rural-urban as spacial constructs, but emphasises that the social spheres can exist independent of the spacial sphere (Ibid: 39–41). Accordingly rural and urban often merge into one social space, which is formed through survival strategies and organisations – Steinbrink uses the term 'translocal livelihood systems'–of the marginalised population.

The present paper does not directly focus on such kind of 'translocal communities' and can not completely abandon a distinction between the city and the countryside. Nevertheless, Steinbrink's concept offers an alternative perspective for thinking of rural-urban linkages which can be very useful in the attempt to understand the situation and changes of the rural-urban relations in the broader region of Hyderabad without sticking to a strict division of the localities, but rather keeping the focus on the people and their realities of daily life.

2.2 Aspects and patterns of migration

The previous chapter has shown that the approaches for studying and understanding rural and urban areas and their relation are various and part of an ongoing debate. However, it is clear that some kind of movement and exchange has always happened between these areas. Given the fact that migration, even if narrowed down to rural-urban migration, is a phenomenon with uncountable forms and dimensions, this chapter can only provide a very limited insight into studies on rural-urban migration without the attempt of discussing all migration models and theories, but rather with focus on some aspects of the motivations for migration and the maintaining of linkages to the place of origin as well as the situation of migrant communities.

While many studies on rural-urban migration mainly examine the economical dimensions of migration, its social dimensions are at the centre of this paper. Taking into account that social and economic aspects are very much intertwined, it seems useful to consider the 'livelihood' concept. The latter has become quite popular for studying migration and was mentioned earlier in the context of Steinbrink's concept of 'translocal livelihood strategies' – he describes migration as a 'livelihood strategy' (2009: 109). The term 'livelihood' refers to people's ways of living and thus goes beyond analysing the migrants' economical situation and needs, but offers a combined perspective: *A 'livelihoods framework' recognises that households construct their livelihoods within broader socio-economic and physical contexts, using social as well as material assets.* (Staples 2007: 13). This approach allows for considering the agency of the people involved in migration instead of seeing the outer circumstances, which might force them to move as the only causes for the situation. However, a constraint of using this livelihood framework is that it is extremely broad and thus can be used referring to quite a wide range of different scenes. It should therefore not be seen as rigid theoretical model but rather as a methodological tool which offers a possible way of thinking about different ways of living (Ibid: 15).

One debate related to the phenomenon of migration deals with the association of the village/city dichotomy with a 'traditional/'modern' distinction. However, as the debate around modernity is a very complex matter on its own, it would lead too far to discuss details of this controversy here. Nevertheless, it is important to note that extensive studies on that issue have suggested different consequences. While Staples among others points out that migration leads to a breakdown of community ties, other studies find that migration does not necessarily lead to an adaptation of 'modern' lifestyles and decline of 'traditional' societal structures. Shah (1988: 2), for example, challenges the assumption that urbanisation weakens societal structures such as caste and joint-family. Referring to evidence from his research in Gujarat the author points out that these structures play an important role in the life of urban societies, and that they are reinforced through rural-urban migration. In the context of labour migration to industrial factories Fernandes and Chandravarkar, for instance, found in their studies that the societal structures and individual action of the migrants changed only to a certain extent while the traditional organisation and ties with the communities in most of the cases remained strong (Fernandes 1997: 117; Chandravarkar 1994: 397).

These examples show that migration in most of the cases does not simply mean a shift of the location implicating either a complete adaptation to the community at the new place or a straightforward continuity of previous forms of societal organisation. Here the rural-urban linkages play a crucial role. One aspect is that people who migrate directly from the village to the city mostly come through existing links (Shah 1988: 21) which are formed by people from the same community who have already moved to the city and either actively bring other villagers or help newcomers to settle down. Another aspect of rural-urban linkages is that people do rarely migrate in a whole community but more often parts of it or even parts of a family go so that there are normally close ties between those who left for the city and those staying back. Surely there are uncountable constellations and patterns of who migrates and whether and how those people stay in contact with their place of origin. However, some general patterns can be observed. Broadly speaking, the linkages are important for maintaining personal relations, cultural activities as well as for economical reasons. In their study about migrants belonging to the Bhils (a scheduled tribe in central India) Mosse et al. clearly formulate how both the rural and the urban areas are of crucial importance for them: *[The Bhils] face the reality that subsistence farming depends upon migrant earnings (to manage uncertainty, for inputs, investment or dept management), just as 'cultivating' urban work relies on village-based networks.* (Mosse et al. 2007: 194).

This quotation emphasises how dependent some people are on both rural and urban areas and that their way of managing their lives between village and city enforces the close interconnection between the spheres. It is the combination of depending on agriculture and earning money from work in the city, which becomes visible in the pattern of 'circular migration'. The basic pattern of circular migration is that peasants work on the fields during the month of harvest and sowing, which is generally in the season from August till December (Olsen and Murthy 2000). For the rest of the year when the crop is growing they migrate to nearby urban centres and search for a seasonal job. Even though it is not a small-scale phenomenon anymore, there is not much data on circular migration. Deshingkar and Farrington (2009: 85, 86) claim that this form of migration is very much neglected at the policy level.

Having in mind that rural-urban migration very often happens in an attempt to earn a surplus from a job in the city while the employment opportunities in the villages are very limited, it might be assumed that migration usually goes along with (economic) benefit. To take such a correlation for granted is, however, quite misleading as the causality between migration and poverty reduction or social upward mobility has to be examined more carefully.

As Steinbrink points out, there is no consensus whether migration is positive or negative–be it for the general process of development, for the wellbeing of the migrants or for the livelihoods of the people left behind since empirical data confirm both assumptions (2009: 111). To mention examples from Andhra Pradesh, the so called 'Palamau labours' are referred to in some articles as a community which succeeded in gaining a relatively good position through their image as reliable migrant labourers and have thus improved their socio-economic status. Similarly the earth workers from Chittoor are told to have achieved a better living through their strategy of seasonal migration (Deshingkar and Start 2003: 17). Apart from such success stories the vast majority of literature about rural-urban migration paints a picture of a desperate situation the migrants find themselves in. According to Deshingkar and Start (Ibid: 3) the typical picture of a migrant is that of a person trapped in poverty. Empirical data indeed confirms that many people in Andhra Pradesh are still living under the inescapable burden of huge amounts of debts which due to enormous interest rates rise so high that they are forced to work for the moneylender over generations. This extremely exploitative system of bonded labour is officially banned, but nevertheless it is still practiced in many places all over India. As Olsen and Murthy (2000) indicate in their study on bonded labourers from a drought-prone area in Mahabubnagar district in Andhra Pradesh, only from the region around Mahabubnagar town around 50,000 (one third) of the labourers migrating seasonally are bonded labourers. In her study about Nepalese labour migrants in Delhi Thieme (2006: XIII) also argues that most of the migrants are trapped in debts so that the whole community is unable to profit from the migration: *Because of its tie to long-term debt, migrant labour in India is often unproductive and unprofitable for those involved, forcing them to remain migrants for their whole lives.* Thieme further reveals that alcohol consumption is a serious problem and constraint to a better situation of many migrants. She emphasises that many migrants find themselves in a conflicting situation because not consuming alcohol leads to social exclusion (e.g. it secures information about jobs etc.), but consumption of too much alcohol prevents people from saving their money and places a burden on the physical as well as emotional well-being of all people involved (Ibid: 195). This problem of alcohol consumption is not specific to international migration but is described in studies about migrants in Andhra Pradesh as well. In their analysis of reasons for suicide of peasants Reddy and Bhaskar find out that most of the victims in Warangal and Mahabubnagar were also addicted to alcohol and in the district Rayalaseema parts of the wages of casual labourers are paid in the form of alcohol what leads to the situation that even women in these areas consume alcohol regularly (Reddy and Bhaskar 2005: 231). It is interesting, too, that the earlier mentioned village Chittoor seems to owe part of the reason for their relatively better off situation to the fact that they have introduced a complete ban on alcohol (Deshingkar and Start 2003: 26).

The discussed aspects of migration suggest that migrants coming from poor backgrounds in most of the cases lead a life at the margins of the city being socially and economically excluded from the rest of the population. While Thieme argues that their marginality is to some extent compensated through their own kind of organisations and networks within the community and their place of origin (Thieme 2006: 182), Mukherji paints a more depressive picture of filth and urban decay when poverty driven migrants overcrowd the cities. He clearly expresses his pessimistic view concerning the effect of rural-urban migration: *[A]lthough such migration helps to avoid starvation (hence considered desirable to them), it does not improve their economic condition adequately, nor permits their upward social mobility. Further, it leads to a colossal waste of human resources and of national potential. So the migrants are in fact moving from rural to urban poverty.* (Mukherji 2006: 2). In fact, the most recent available data (from 2004–2005) show that in Andhra Pradesh urban poverty (28 %) is considerably higher than rural poverty (11.2 %) (AP-Online 2009-2010: 211). Thus, arguing that slums in cities are a substantial part of the city economy since their population does various jobs which are essential for the daily life of all citizens, many authors claim that theses people as well as their backgrounds should be considered appropriately at the policy level (e.g. Mukherji 2006; Olsen and Murthy 2000; Mosse et al. in Staples 2007: 198).

3 Recent developments in rural and urban areas

3.1 New technologies in the city

Hyderabad has experienced a fast expansion of the information and communication technology (ICT) sector since the 1990s, a process that is very much pushed forward by the state government of Andhra Pradesh. This development is examined in the present chapter with the aim to identify its impact on people from rural areas.

Due to economic liberalisation, India has attracted numerous ICT-related companies since the post-1992 period. Many of them settled in Bangalore (Mathew et al. (ed.) 2005: 77). Likewise, a technology park has been established at the outskirts of Hyderabad. In this so-called *'Hi-Tec city'* (Hyderabad Information Technology and Engineering Consultancy City), the *'Cyber Towers'* alone offer 8,50,000 sqft of office space (Chowdary 2002: 3887). An area of about 52 sqkm around this *'Hi-Tec City'* has been carved out as a separate administrative entity with the name *"Cyberabad"* (Ramachandraiah 2003: 1195). The majority of the services provided here is for export since many ICT companies (mainly from the US) have outsourced some tasks for which India is ideal, regarding that there is a huge English speaking work force willing to accept low wages. One of the services done in Hyderabad is, for example, medical transcription for the US and Mexico (Mir et al. 2000: 6).

This recent boom of the ICT sector is interpreted as an entirely positive trend by some. In an article titled *'The power to make India shine'* (Front matter (EPW) 2004) the policies of Andhra Pradesh's chief minister Naidu are outlined as concentrating mainly on the development of the ICT sector (including an e-government project) through which he wants to archive rapid development and employment with the aim to make the state the best destination for potential investors. These policies are presented in an extremely positive light suggesting that considerable success is visible and that *[Naidu] has worked hard to modernise the hitherto largely rural state through information technology.* (Front matter (EPW) 2004: 962). Similarly, Chowdary (2002) is convinced that the government of Andhra Pradesh is right in focusing on technological development to achieve rapid progress that includes everybody. In sharp contrast to such statements, others point out their serious concerns about these policies. For example, the governmental document *'Vision 2020'*, which outlines policy goals including the model of e-governance, is harshly criticised and found to ignore the most urgent problems such as poverty and landlessness (e.g. Bandyopadhyay 2001; R.V. 1999). R.V. even points out: *Overall, the document leaves one with the feeling that the chief minister is more comfortable with economic growth than human development.* (R.V. 1999: 392).

These contrasting interpretations of recent developments in Andhra Pradesh and the above-mentioned government priorities pose the question of whether or what kind of influence the discussed policies have on the poor part of the population including those from the villages. While Muklund (2003: 703) identifies a trend of declining disparities between different social sectors, indicating that the effects of development are beginning to reach the backward parts of the population, many studies find that the poor people are left out by government policies and do not benefit from ICT development. Many are excluded from new opportunities as some kind of degree and English skills are definitely necessary for getting a job in the ICT sector. Consequently, the huge majority of the poor population do not benefit from this kind of technology-focused development, nor do they get any support or benefits from government programmes designed for poverty alleviation (Bandyopadhyay 2001: 902). Ramachandraiah even argues in an article on IT and social development: *This whole process is widening the gap between areas that are regarded as economically 'viable' and those that are not.* (2003: 1196). Finding that the focus on urban IT development has led to a neglect of rural areas, he suggests that social development has to be included into the process. Otherwise, a whole part of society will be left behind (Ibid).

3.2 New technologies and development in rural areas

Having seen that ICT-related new technologies do not directly reach the poor and alliterated sections of the population, but rather widen the gap within society, this chapter focuses on developments that are brought about by new technologies in the rural areas. It will also discuss the call for projects that consider and build upon local strategies to improve the situation of the villagers. The analysis shall help to shed some light on the needs and perspectives of the rural population as well as the possible shortcomings of such projects.

Some people actually believe that positive change in the situation of the rural population is happening directly through the influence of new technologies. As Chelikani (2010) strongly emphasises in his book *'Rural transformations'*, he is convinced that new technologies are 'spilling over' to the countryside very fast, bringing about positive change for rural livelihoods. His assumption seems to be that development policies should 'modernise' at any cost, making the villages 'modern' in terms of access to modern facilities, material and knowhow so that the standard of living and connectivity to the rest of the world become comparable to urban standards.

Acknowledging that the kind of development needed in rural areas cannot just be brought from the outside or the cities and transform the villages into urban sites, many authors formulate the demand for effective projects and initiatives which are suitable for the local context (see e.g. Mosse 2005; Parthasarathy 1995). It is obvious that introducing new technologies alone does not automatically bring about development. However, even very well-planned projects that are designed for the specific situation on the ground and involve local people may sometimes fail out of purely social reasons. For instance, in her article on a weaver community in the South Indian town of Pattamadai, Venkatesan (2010) describes how a development worker who had lived and worked with the people for some years, closely observing their working conditions, failed in her attempt to introduce a more ergonomic loom. Interestingly, the reason why the weavers rejected the new technology that could have enhanced their physical well-being as well as their occupational success had to do with the fact that they considered the occupation of weaving as socially very low so that they only did it if they had no other option (Venkatesan 2009: 172). This example clearly shows that social concepts and the status of people within society also play a crucial role for the success of development projects. Baviskar's (1997) work even suggests that projects employing new technologies, but too heavily relying on a nostalgic assumption of 'romantic village life' are likely to fail as they may not properly reflect the perspectives and wishes of the villagers.

As another concrete example of how urgent but at the same time complex the implementation of technology-based development projects is, energy is an interesting field. It obviously represents a rural-urban disparity and underlines the strong need for improving the supply system and access to new technologies. However, the energy sector also exemplifies the difficulties of how and where to start. One of the major dilemmas is created by the situation that grid energy is not very reliable in quality and quantity but so much subsidised that people pay almost nothing and might thus not be able or willing to invest into something like renewable energy. The importance to find out what people really need and want in their specific situation, i.e. to include them into the process, is crucial for the efficiency or failure of such projects (e.g. Ashworth 1980). Vidyarthi (1985: 1957), for instance, finds that the social aspects of energy projects are often ignored: *[K]nowledge about energy related technology greatly exceeds knowledge about the problems which the technology is meant to solve.* As a detailed analysis of energy projects would go beyond the scope of this paper, it shall suffice here to bear in mind that the power sector is one of the areas crucial for rural development, but at the same time extremely complex to tackle – not only because of technological but also because of social constraints.

4 Rural-urban linkages in the broader region of Hyderabad–Empirical study

In this chapter the findings of my empirical research in Hyderabad are presented and discussed. I have conducted ten expert interviews with the aim to gain some insights into the rural-urban relations in this specific area. The interview partners are all in some way or the other, through their occupations or extra-occupational activities, in contact with rural areas, people from rural areas or issues related to urban migration or planning. Dr. Chelikani is the president of a citizen's welfare association. Prof. S. Kumar is head of the department of urban and regional planning in the *Jawaharlal Nehru Architecture and Fine Arts University (JNAFA)*. Mrs. Kannan is founder of the NGO *Right to Walk Foundation*. Mr. J. Kumar is as human rights activist and works with the organisation *Campaign for Housing and Tenurial Rights*. Prof. Rao works in the Energy Conservation mission. Mrs. Reddy is active in the Society for Preservation of Environment and Quality of Life. Mr. Narayan is an architect. Mr. Vikram is involved in the NGO *M. Venkatarangaiya Foundation*, which tries to combat child labour. Mr. Raju runs the *Short Stay Home* for desperate women and children from rural areas, and Dr. Ramachandraiah is active in the *Forum for Better Public Transport in Hyderabad*.

The following sections present the perspectives, knowledge and assumptions of the informants on different aspects of the broad topic of rural-urban linkages. I have collected this information in semi-structured interviews organised in four sections covering the intensity of the linkages, the motivations of people to move from rural to urban areas and vice versa, requirements for better opportunities for rural areas and the role that village-city links and new technologies may play in village development.

4.1 How intense are the rural-urban linkages between the core city of Hyderabad and its rural surroundings?

In order to estimate the intensity of rural-urban linkages, factors such as the extent of migration, the nature and frequency of contact and exchange of goods between the two areas, as well as the duration of the stay in the city are discussed. Starting with the interview partners themselves, it is interesting that most of them have some kind of personal relation to rural areas. While three of them originally come from villages, three more have parents from the countryside, and the majority have contact to rural areas through their work. The assumptions of those who tried a guess on the percentage of Hyderabad citizens who have migrated from the surrounding areas reach up to 75 % (Rao). With regard to some villages, an outmigration of 80 % is estimated (Raju).

The varying information about who normally migrates shows that different patterns are possible. Most often men migrate (Narayan, Ramachandrayan), sometimes taking along their families later (S. Kumar, Rao). Elders and sometimes children are often left behind (Reddy, Kannan, Kumar, Vikram). Some informants emphasise that it also depends on the distance and on the place of origin–entire families normally only come from nearby areas (Chelikani) or drought-prone regions (Reddy, Kumar). In the common case that parts of the family or relatives stay back in the village, most informants are sure that the latter maintain close contact as family ties are very important in the Indian society (e.g. Kannan). Chalikani calls this phenomenon a *'sentimental link'*. While estimates about the frequency of contact vary, most of the informants mention mobile phones as the most important medium used in both city and villages for staying in contact. Vikram even claims that interaction is increasing as the spread of mobile phones makes it easier to keep in touch without spending much money or time on travelling. Maintaining close contact can be an important mechanism encouraging and supporting an ongoing flow of migrants: *They come normally through family links, somebody who stays already here will accommodate them. So they don't come as an unknown individual, but they come through reference, caste reference or community reference, some kind of link. And in fact people who are here, they go and then get others. You can say they are collected from the villages.* (Chelikani). Social obligations and religious festivals play a crucial role in reinforcing strong ties within the communities even if they live in different places. Among such functions, weddings are mentioned the most; the estimated number of festivals for which migrants go back to the villages varies from two to six or eight per year (e.g. Vikram). In Andhra Pradesh the two main festivals are Sankranti, which is celebrated in January for the harvest season especially in the coastal area, and Dushera in October, which is celebrated mainly in the Telagana district (J. Kumar). According to Ramachandraiah, around two million people leave the city during Sankranti to celebrate in their villages so that it looks like undeclared holidays in Hyderabad. Interestingly, agricultural work, which is the other main reason to go back, is mentioned much less than cultural functions (e.g. Kannan). Other occasions for going back to the village are illness of the migrant if it is not too serious (Vikram), and election times (J. Kumar).

Concerning the duration of the stay in the city, the claim that migrants do not want to stay for long because *people do not sacrifice their family for earning money* (Chelikani) and therefore prefer seasonal jobs, stands against the assumption that they normally do not go back to stay in the village permanently but try to become permanent in the city (Reddy, Kannan, Ramachandraiah). While both of these tendencies might exist, a pattern of seasonal migration seems to be common among people in agricultural occupations (Chelikani, S. Kumar, Narayan): *they live in two places many times, they come to the city when the crops are growing, but when the crops have to be harvested or sown they go back to their villages. [...] Probably they spend three month in the villages and the rest of the time in the city.* (Narayan). Vikram outlines a similar pattern of circular migration among construction workers, who usually stay in the city for around 60 work days and then have a break of four to six days during which they go back to their villages. However, the scenario might be different in the case of young people. As Ramachandraiah suggests, those young people who come to the city for IT training do normally not go back to the villages after completing their training. Chelikani assumes changing attitudes among the second generation of migrants, who are probably more comfortable with living in the city than their parents and slowly abandon their linkages to the village. Similarly, there is no uniform pattern according to which migrants move back to the village for their retirement (or not). While Vikram argues that the hard work they do can only be done up to a certain age and then they go back to the village, other informants assume that the trend of going to the villages for retirement will only start later (Chelikani, Reddy). On the one hand, the city becomes increasingly noisy and polluted so that people wish to spend their post-retirement life in a calm village (Rao). On the other hand, there are some issues such as insufficient health care and lack of other modern facilities that prevent people from moving back to their villages (Narayan, Ramachandraiah).

In most cases, close contact between migrants in the city and their relatives in the village goes along with an exchange of goods between these areas. According to most of the informants, the main subject of transfer is money, which people send or bring back to the villages depending on their income (Chelikani, S. Kumar, Kannan, Raju, Vikram, J. Kumar, Ramachandraiah, Reddy). Rao even gives a concrete number: *Generally they try to send at least 50 % of their savings to the village.* In terms of money transfers, many informants mention the system of 'money order', which is offered by post offices. However, they have different information on how much this system is used or whether it is already outdated (e.g. Narayan). In some cases people send back money only for paying back debts from a money lender (Narayan).

In terms of non-financial exchange, there is a certain extent of basic food transfer, which is mainly directed from the village to the city. Migrants may take along local specialities or food that is cheaper in the village such as rice, daal, masala, pickles, vegetables, grains and sweets (Kannan, Raju, Rao). Ramachandraiah points out that there are even well-established courier services and agencies for the delivery of goods and food items from villages to the city (for instance, he gets mangos sent by his family via normal busses) as well as informal networks of friends and relatives that transport things in both directions. However, it is stated that there is no need to bring much to the villages because most things are available there, too, except for high level facilities (Ramachandrayana).

4.2 What are the motivations to migrate and is the picture changing due to the ICT Boom in the city?

The most mentioned reason for migration to the city is the lack of job opportunities in the villages (e.g. Raju, Vikram, Ramachandraiah, Rao). Moreover, the lack of educational facilities (Reddy, Narayan, Rao) as well as the shortage of water in some areas are among the crucial factors that make people leave the village (Reddy, S. Kumar). The fact that the situation in drought prone areas has become very desperate has, according to Reddy, let to a change in the patterns of migration. While in former times the migrants usually had a double base, since they didn't want to sell their land in the village, a lot of migrants nowadays come from far away regions. Since the living conditions have become extremely bad in these regions, they totally abandon their villages, sell the land and come to the city without a place to stay. Another crucial factor is the alcohol consumption. As Raju explains, alcohol addiction of men in rural areas is a severe problem, which ruins whole families and forces them to migrate. Ramachandraiah, points out that *There is too much of liquor consumption in the villages which is destroying rural livelihood especially in the low income group*. He even claims that this is in fact encouraged by the government to make money out of the taxes.

As S. Kumar argues, these so called 'push factors' in the rural areas are stronger than the 'pull factors' of the city because it is mainly poverty induced migration. However, some of the informants also mention the wide spread idea that you get employment and a good living in the city (S. Kumar). Moreover, the desire for a higher social status, which you can achieve through living in a metropolis with a prestigious address (Kannan) is also an important reason for people to migrate. Vikram argues that this has to do with the phenomenon that the myth of success stories–it could be only one example of someone from the village who settled down happily in the city–circulates and is kept alive as a vivid memory despite many negative examples.

Apart from a general need or wish to migrate, some informants point out that there might also be concrete purposes for what people want to earn money in the city. This could be for building or renovating the house (Chelikani), buying land in the village or paying back debts (J. Kumar). Such kind of intentions clearly indicate the wish of many people to keep their base in the village or even to invest in it – be it for themselves or their relatives. This aspect of the village-city link fits into the earlier mentioned picture that migrants normally maintain strong ties to their villages, which is very much emphasised by the informants.

Resulting from the different reasons for moving to the city and thus different aspirations of the life in the city the jobs migrants do are also various. The most obvious factor, which the occupation depends on, is the educational level of the migrants. Since the vast majority of the people from rural sides has a low level of education, the informants declare that the jobs they generally do in the city are unskilled services like construction work, watchmen, security guards, drivers (private, rickshaw, truck or bus), domestic servants, electricians, plumbers, workers in the malls, cleaners, coconut sellers, work in tanneries, vegetable selling, biscuit selling, work in sweet shops, meat shops and small business like beedi rolling, etc. These jobs are typical occupations in the informal sector, which is according to S. Kumar the domain of the migrants in the city. As most of the informants mention, these migrants typically live in slums of which the city accommodates 1,900 (J. Kumar). This huge working force of unskilled migrants is very much needed by the citizens: *Uneducated people come here more because [. . .] city people need cooks, drivers, nannies, gardeners, watchmen and various other things which many other countries in the West cannot afford.* (Rao). In the worst case unskilled migrants are not able to get any such kind of job but end up, as Reddy observes, living on the streets of the city doing 'nothing' but trying to survive on a day to day basis without enough education and ideas to change this situation by themselves. The counterpart of those migrants in an extremely desperate situation are those who have more education and come to the city for skilled jobs such as government related jobs, political activities, IT related jobs (Ramachandraiah), accountants or shopkeepers (Rao).

Most of the informants emphasise that education becomes more and more important, even among very poor people (e.g. Raju, Narayan, Ramachandraiah). Hence some people come to the city in order to get their skills upgraded with the hope of better job chances. As many of the informants suggest, a new wave of motivation to aim at higher education and English skills seems to have started among young people from the rural areas (Kannan, Ramachandraiah, Rao). This rather recent development is closely connected to the vast expansion of the ICT sector in the city (Ramachandraiah). Rao, however, suggests that only very few people actually get jobs directly in this sector after being trained in the IT training centres. It is on the other hand emphasised by Ramachandraiah that nowadays hundreds of young people come to Hyderabad for such kind of training and then get IT-related jobs either in the city itself or abroad. According to Narayan, such kind of training centres are even put up in towns on a small scale.

Apart from jobs directly related to the ICT sector most of the informants suggest that the boom of this sector has some kind of influence on the job situation for migrants from the villages. It is observed that this boom creates a lot of 'side jobs' in the unskilled labour and service sector. Besides the most apparent need for labour in the construction of the new offices, residences, malls, etc. Rao, for example, explains that people in ICT jobs develop a need for services like: drivers, gardeners, shop keepers, nannies, nurse e.g. Narayan, who claims that the IT development is very hyped up, although not even two per cent of the overall population of the country is directly involved in the IT sector, argues in a similar direction that the spending capacity of these people is very high so their consumption creates a disproportional number of new jobs (Narayan).

Regarding the future development of the migration patterns, the assumptions presented by the majority of the informants suggest that–unlike to Chelikani's theory of a slowing down of the migration at the present as well as in the future – the urban migration will further increase (Reddy, S. Kumar, Kannan, Raju, Vikram, J. Kumar). Giving concrete numbers Vikram suggests that from around 60 % of people living in the village at the present it will come down to 40 %. He sees the main challenge in countering this trend in providing diverse opportunities through creating more cities rather than one big city: *The system should be more decentralised.* Rao, who also sees a strong need to discourage further migration, formulates an obligation of the government to handle the migration issue: *Migration should reverse. It is the duty of every government in every country to reduce the migration irrespective whether it is India, China, Germany or wherever it is, because the cities should not be burdened. And it is morally unethical that a person can not enjoy the same quality of service in his village like his fellow people are enjoying in the city.*

4.3 What is needed to create better perspectives in the villages?

As it has become clear that a huge proportion of urban migration has to do with a lack of opportunities and insufficient facilities in the rural areas, this section analyses the informant's suggestions concerning the most urgent requirements for creating better perspectives in the villages.

According to what they identified as the major problems in the villages and the main reason for people to migrate to the city, the informants suggest most of all a strong need for the creation of job opportunities (Chelikani, Narayan). Interestingly, S. Kumar is the only one who mentions the *National Rural Employment Guarantee Act (NREGA)* that has been promoted by the Congress and is in force since 2006 (as part of the eleventh five year plan). He points out that this act is designed in order to bring employment to the villages and thus reduce the 'pull factor' and with it the migration to the city. However, he does not know how successful it is. Other urgent issues are the improvement of educational institutions and health facilities as well as other basic facilities (like housing, access to clean drinking water, etc.) (Reddy, Narayan, Raju, Ramachandraiah). Besides, a development of the infrastructure has to be encouraged (Kannan, Vikram) and the government should reduce the liquor consumption (Ramachandraiah).

As one possible idea for projects, which could help to improve the situation in the rural areas, Kannan suggests that a 'local tourism' should be developed and encouraged. She is convinced that every village has something unique what should be maintained and made use of in a way, which is suitable to the respective communities. Following her claim that Indian villages are completely neglected, she assumes that a rediscovering of the beauty and original prosperity of the rural areas for eco-friendly tourism could help to stop the trend of the decay of the villages. This could also create jobs and perspectives for the rural population.

Turning to the example of energy provision, it is pointed out by many of the interview partners that reliable energy provision is very important for all aspects of live in the village, but most crucial on the agricultural level. If there is no power for running the pump sets to water the plants the whole cycle becomes affected (Narayan). S. Kumar even claims that there is hardly any power in many villages. He identifies the power sector as clearly representing the unequal distribution between city and village, which becomes clearly visible in the reality that the villages are neglected while metros rush in the cities (S. Kumar). Most of the informants agree on the fact that the villagers do not get good quality power in the allocated time. There are often break downs of electricity in the villages–up to 80 % power cuts are suggested by Raju, which are particularly frequent during summer (Ramachandraiah). Moreover, the supply and the voltage is extremely unpredictable. As a result Chelikani assumes that half of the energy is wasted in agriculture because of bad pipes and material and because it comes so irregularly that people just leave the switch on when they go to bed for example.

Regarding the role of the government, it is claimed by some that they generally show indifference. J. Kumar and Vikram argue that the government does something in this regard, though not enough. The problem of bad implementation of projects and insufficient maintenance of the system are mentioned as serious constraints. As some informants emphasise, the main problem of implementation of renewable energies, for instance, lies in the fact that the power for rural areas is highly subsidised. Narayan formulates this problem as follows: *Once they get free power then who would go for solar? It may sound funny, but unless you reduce the subsidies you can not increase other technologies.* The same argumentation leads Chelikani to put the blame on the democratic system. He argues that it has created the conflict that the politicians, who need the rural population as vote bank, have very limited possibilities to reduce the subsidies on electricity for enabling more implementation of alternative energies.

All in all, most of the informants see renewable energy as an important option for the future (e.g. Chelikani, Narayan, Kannan, J. Kumar). As S. Kumar points out, an implementation of renewable energies is happening in some cases, but more is badly needed and could also provide job opportunities in the villages. While most of the informants highlight solar energy as very important, Vikram as the only one expresses his doubt in the efficiency of this technology at the current stage. However, most of the others who see the implementation of solar and other renewable energies as possible perspective for the future, also emphasise that this development still needs a lot of time as well as more research and awareness about the matter (e.g. Ramachandraiah, J. Kumar).

4.4 Which role do new technologies and the city-village link play for the village development?

Having analysed some important aspects of the village-city linkages and the situation and perspectives of the villages, the question comes up whether these personal links do have an impact on the village development and in case they do, what kind of changes can be observed through this form of contact between the village and the city? The assumptions of the informants on these questions are outlined in the present section together with their views concerning the influence of new technologies on the rural population.

Overall the assumptions of the interview partners concerning the influence of the rural-urban linkages and new technologies on the village development differ a lot. S. Kumar, for instance, very optimistically points out that in most of the cases the people get new ideas in the city and implement these (such as water filters for example) in their respective villages which is slowly changing and improving the situation and living conditions there. According to Ramachandraiah, some kind of investment in the villages happens, though rather on the personal or family scale: *Some people these days are showing interest in buying some plots of land in the villages. Maybe if they require in post retirement, maybe next generation...* J. Kumar and Chelikani also emphasise that migrants often invest in land or renovation of their house in the villages, which according to Narayan, brings up the economy of all worker in the village. As J. Kumar argues, some migrants also do something for the general welfare in their villages. This could be in form of supporting schools and panchayat systems, picking up children and bringing them to hospitals for example (J. Kumar).

Apart from such concrete measures which some migrants might take, there are also slow changes that happen through the rural-urban linkages: *The flow of information back to the village makes a lot of difference in changing the attitude in the village.* (Ramachandraiah). He has, for example, observed the phenomenon that the people become more confident in sending their children to the city for higher studies. In the case of the women from the 'Short stay home' Raju explains that their temporarily stay in the city often has two positive effects. Sometimes they start new small business alone or together with others in the village and the women usually get much more respect since they are themselves earning now on the basis of the education they have got in the city. A growing interest in (good) education is mentioned as a result of the contact to the city by many informants, (e.g. Rao, Chalikani). An increasing interest in education that seems to be apparent even among very poor people has been mentioned in the context of the motivations for people to migrate to the city (Section 4.2). However, adding another aspect to this picture, Reddy offers a much more critical insight into that topic when she talks about changes that occur through the contact to the city. She states that the importance of education for the children is only observable among a certain level of migrants, but definitely not everybody. Moreover, she points out that education stands in direct conflict with the 'real job' of the people. To make it more clear Reddy tells the story of how she once on a visit in a village met a young boy who was the only one in the village not actually working but sitting under a tree. He was wearing a jeans and when she asked him: *Why are you sitting here not doing something?* he answered: *I have studied up to class ten so I cannot work in the village.* This example illustrates that the there is no direct causality between more education and 'modern ideas'–whether they come from the city of the village–and an improvement in the rural livelihoods, but the reality is much more complex. Chelikani, although he emphasises: *I try to persuade that only through rural and urban linkages we can develop the rural area.*, similarly to Reddy points out that through living in the city and experiencing the 'urban lifestyle' people dissociate themselves from the village life: *In an urban context the human being is transformed by education, by styles of life... They cannot even drink the water in a village and they cannot communicate with the former generation in the language they learned.* Even though Chlikani is convinced that this leads to a weakening and disturbance of the community links, he–rather than seeing this as problematic development–speaks enthusiastically about the fact that the villages are more open now. Hence, according to him, new ideas and life styles are penetrating the village communities much more easily and changes happen faster.

As discussed in the literature research about new technologies in rural areas (Section 3.2) referring to Chelikani's book, he is convinced that the urban facilities and with that a lot of new opportunities are coming to the villages. Thus, the trend of 'urbanising' the villages will over the long run discourage more rural-urban migration: *This makes people stay there because the technology comes to their door and they can work there and earn more money.* Other informants, too, point out that new technologies like basic communication and entertainment facilities (TV, mobiles, internet etc.) have established in the rural areas (e.g. Narayan). Thus, Vikram argues that the rural population is exposed to new ideas because they see the 'new life style' in the TV, therefore they do not need people coming back from the city and bringing such kind of ideas. Rao even states: *In fact the people in the rural areas know more about the products [referring to his solar lamps] because they have more time to watch whereas the people in the city are busy, stuck in a traffic jam or somewhere else so they don't have much time to watch TV.* He, however, admits that indirectly the city-village link does help to improve the situation in the villages through a growing consumption.

In sharp contrast to describing the information flow from the city to the villages and the increasing spread of new technologies in the rural areas as a positive development, Reddy emphasises that this whole development as well as new technologies in the villages (such as TV, mobiles with visuals, films e.g.) leads to a lot of dissatisfaction. She claims that the progress which happens through new technologies does not include all people but in fact has very negative effects on a huge number of people. Starting from talking about this unsatisfying development, Reddy expresses her concerns about the kind of 'development' she observes in general. The need for labour in the urban areas leads to an extraction of unskilled labour from the villages, but this does not lead to an improvement of these people's lives. Thus, the linkages encourage greater migration but the people in fact end up somehow surviving in the city. They can not cope with the city life and do not experience a positive change in quality of life: *We have taken a whole country which had opportunities to do so many things, traditional things what their parents did [...]. We have converted it all into what is called a 'backward class' and told them that you do not need to study, you do not need to work, we will provide for you. And so we have converted all these people into becoming a dependent community.* (Reddy). Kannan, too, is not sure whether the linkages can support the village development, but sees it mainly as a clash because people who have migrated to the city look down to the villagers and do not give anything back to the village. Concerning the influence of new technologies in rural areas Kannan warns about the dangers of the use of pesticides, for example. In this context she points at problematic effects of a development, which does not include the whole population: *What are the costs of development? Who is paying for it? It's the poorest who pay for it.*

4.5 Discussion of the findings from the literature research and the empirical study

The analysis of different aspects of rural-urban linkages through literature research and interviews has let to a range of findings, which are discussed in this section. Beginning with the debate on a rural-urban divide the claim of some authors that the areas should not be seen in contrast to each other has been confirmed by findings from the empirical study. The interview partners describe a vivid contact, movement and exchange between these areas, which necessarily cause a mutual influence and thus make the thinking of a dichotomy pointless. The fact that people usually maintain very strong ties within their communities is evident in a frequent contact and a system of recruiting and accommodating members of the community as well as in the very common pattern of circular migration. This way of managing their lives in a sphere beyond regional borders proves the theory of translocal livelihood strategies by Steinbrink. However, some statements and argumentations of the informants build on a sharp distinction between city and village. As soon as it comes to issues of development, most of the interview partners claim that the rural sites are very much neglected and that there is an unequal distribution between these areas.

Concerning the migration patterns it is suggested in the literature as well as by most of the informants that usually families do not migrate as a whole, but rather in different steps or only parts of the family go leaving the others behind. Moreover, the general conclusion from the literature that there is no clear consensus whether migration brings about a positive change in the socio-economic situation of the people involved has been reflected in the statements of the informants as well. As suggested by many authors, the migrants often end up in a very desperate situation. Similarly, most interview partners describe the living and working conditions of the vast majority of migrants in the city as extremely unfortunate. In the context of poverty induced migration the phenomenon of bonded labour in Andhra Pradesh is discussed in the literature, while the informants do not directly talk about that. However, some of them mention that one of the reasons for which some migrants have to earn money in the city is in order to pay back debts. This could be private debt as well but regarding the scale of the bonded labour described by Olsen and Murthy it is likely that the informants refer to the same phenomenon.

Broadly, the reasons given for migration in the literature as well as in the interviews cover the same aspects. The lack of job opportunities and basic facilities in the villages are definitely the major issues. The problem of too much alcohol consumption was mentioned in the literature analysis in the context of the situation of migrant communities and the high rates of suicides of peasants because of agricultural crises. Some informants, furthermore, claim that alcohol consumption–in some areas even supported by the government–sometimes destroys families and communities and forces people to migrate. A certain idea of modernity also plays a role in the motivations for urban migration. This aspect has been mentioned in the literature analysis without going much into detail of the debate whether city and village can be associated with 'modern' and 'traditional' structures of the population. To assume such a clear relation is definitely a simplification–especially if we consider the former analysed intensity of rural-urban linkages. However, it has become clear in the statements of some informants that many people actually have the idea that simply through moving to the city they can become part of a 'modern' lifestyle which is considered to be more prestigious than the life in the village (Kannan).

The assumptions of the interview partners concerning the typical occupation of migrants in the city confirm what has also been described by the discussed authors. Migrants generally do any kind of job that can be done with a very low level of education, such as unskilled labour in the construction sector and domestic service. Thus, it is generally assumed that the boom of the ICT sector in the city has not created new job opportunities for many migrants from rural areas. Some informants, however, argue that besides the trend that many young people come to the city for higher education or IT training the fast growth of the ICT-related business creates a huge demand for unskilled workers. As some informants emphasise, those people who work in ICT-related jobs generate a disproportional amount of jobs such as drivers, cooks, nannies, etc. All in all, it is assumed a problematic development that the concentration of the state government for bringing about a fast progress in Andhra Pradesh lies most of all on expanding the ICT sector. In the literature as well as in the interviews some people argue that this focus ignores the most urgent problems of a lot of people, especially in the rural areas and thus leads to a widening of the gap in society. Hence, a need of an orientation towards the rural areas and the basic needs of the people is formulated by many authors and is also the prevailing concern among the interview partners.

Turning to the example of the energy sector, most of the informants have agreed that this is a problematic field in rural areas that urgently needs improvement. This claim was also found in the literature research. It is in the literature as well as in most of the interviews suggested that renewable energies such as solar can be a future option for the rural areas. It is nevertheless the concern of most informants that very high subsidies on electricity make the implementation of alternative methods very difficult. This confirms the claim of some authors that projects aiming at implementing new technologies have to take the local situation into account.

To conclude, it has become obvious in both, literature research and empirical study that it is not possible to generalise the effects that the linkages between city and villages as well as new technologies have on the rural population and their relation to the city. The empirical study has made clear that the influence of people who come back from the city varies between contributing with huge investments in the village development and an attitude of not wanting to be involved with the problems in the village at all. The discussion of the influence of new technologies on the rural population in the literature rather focused on the possible conflicts of implementing such projects. Some interview partners, however, also talk about the positive and negative effects of the nowadays extremely fast spread of new technologies. It is on the one hand assumed that through this development the rural population will soon become part of the progress and economical growth. On the other hand substantial concerns are expressed about such kind of 'development', which does not include everybody equally, but exploits huge parts of the population, enforced through the rural-urban linkages.

5 Conclusion

Having analysed some aspects of rural-urban relations in the broader region of Hyderabad, this paper has tried to answer the question of how rural-urban linkages function and which influences new technologies have on these relations. The examination of literature on these issues as well as the conversations with experts from the region itself have shown that the topic is extremely huge and cannot be done away with in one comprehensive answer.

Throughout the analysis the focus has been on the rural population and its relation to the city. With regard to the question of how the linkages function, it is found that with the urban migration that happens on a large scale very strong ties between village and city are maintained in most cases. In fact, some people build their livelihoods on revenues from both areas. Whether people leave their village temporarily or permanent, as long as parts of their community stay back, they usually keep a frequent contact and return to the village for all major cultural functions such as religious festivals and weddings.

Concerning the influences of new technologies, the example of the ICT boom in Hyderabad has shown that this development has encouraged more urban migration but without substantially improving the situation of many people. Since the enormous growth of the ICT sector in India is a quite recent phenomenon, the social side effects of this development have not been much studied yet. More research on the matter could explore to what extent an increased focus on education may enable even poor people to access skilled jobs in the ICT sector. Moreover, further research on rural-urban linkages–from a more in-depth perspective that includes the voices of villagers and migrants–could provide a closer insight into how village-city linkages work and how they may support village development.

References

Ashworth, J. 1980. "Technology Diffusion through Foreign Assistance: Making Renewable Energy Sources Available to the World's Poor" *Policy Sciences* 11(3): 241–261.

AP-Online. 2009–2010. "Andhra Pradesh Socio-Economic Survey Report 2009-2010." www.aponline.gov.in/Apportal/AP%20Govt%20Information/APES%20New/APSES.html [10-09-10].

Bandyopadhyay, D. 2001. "Andhra Pradesh: Looking beyond "Vision 2020"." *Economic and Political Weekly* 36(11): 900–903.

Baviskar, A. 1997. "Tribal Politics and Discourses of Environmentalism." *Contributions to Indian Sociology* 31(2): 195–223.

Chandavarkar, R. 1994. *The Origins of Industrial Capitalism in India: Business strategies and the working class in Bombay 1900-1940*. Mumbai: Cambridge University Press.

Chelikani, R.V.B.J. 2010. "Rural transformations: A rapid survey of current trends." Hyderabad: Kala Jyothi Process Ptv. Ltd.

Chowdarty, T. H. 2002. "Information Technology for Development: Necessary Conditions." *Economic and Political Weekly* 37(38): 3886–3889.

Deshingkar, P. and J. Farrington (eds.). 2009. *Circular Migration and Multilocational Livelihood Strategies in Rural India*. New Delhi: Oxford University Press.

Deshingkar, P. and D. Start. 2003. *Seasonal Migration for Livelihoods in India: Coping, Accumulation and Exclusion*. Working Paper 220.

Fernandes, L. 1997. *Producing workers: the politics of gender, class, and culture in the Calcutta jute mills*. Philadelphia: University of Pennsylvania Press.

Front Matter. 2004. "The power to make India shine." *Economic and Political Weekly* 39(9): 857–964.

Ghosh, S. 1991. *Economic development in India: urban bias or rural bias?* New Delhi: Deep & Deep.

Greatandhra.com. 2008. "Reddy launches HMDA replacing HUDA." www.greatandhra.com/viewnews.php?id=9425&cat=&scat=4 [10-09-10].

Lipton, M. 1977. *Why poor people stay poor: Urban bias in world development*. London: Temple Smith.

Lynch, O. M. 1992. "Rural Cities in India: Continuities and Discontinuities." In *Urban Sociology in India: Reader and Source Book.* edited by Rao, M. S. A., (first publ. 1974). New Delhi: Sangam Books.

Mathew, K. S., M. Singh and J. Varkey (eds.). 2005. *Migration in South India.* New Delhi: Shipra publications.

Mir, A., B. Mathew and R. Mir. 2000. "The Codes of Migration: Contours of the Global Software Labor Market." *Cultural Dynamics* 12(5): 5–33.

Mosse et al. 2007. "Vulnerability in the city: Adivasi seasonal labour migrants in western India" In *Livelihoods at the margins: surviving the city.* edited by Staples. California: Left Coast Press.

Mosse, D. 2005. *Cultivating development: Ethnography of Aid Policy and Practice.* London: Pluto Press.

Mukherji, S. 2006. *Migration and urban decay: Asian experiences.* Jaipur: Rawat Publications.

Mukund, K. 2003. "Regional Disparities." *Economic and Political Weekly* 38(8): 703–704.

Olsen, W. K. and R.V. Ramana Murthy. 2000. "Contract Labour and Bondage in Andhra Pradesh (India)." *The journal of social work* 1(2).

Parthasarathy, G. 1995. "Public Intervention and Rural Poverty: Case of Non-Sustainable Reduction in Andhra Pradesh." *Economic and Political Weekly* 30(41/42): 2573–2586.

Pocock, D. 1960. "Sociologies: Urban and rural." In *Urban Sociology in India: Reader and Source Book.* 1992. edited by Rao, M.S.A., (first publ. 1974). New Delhi: Sangam Books.

R. V. 1999. "Andhra's 'Vision 2020'" *Economic and Political Weekly* 34(7): 391–392.

Ramachandraiah, C. 2003. "Information Technology and Social Development." *Economic and Political Weekly* 38(12/13): 1192–1197.

Reddy, V. A. and G. Bhaskar (eds.). 2005. *Rural Transformation in India. The Impact of Globalisation.* New Delhi: New Century Publication.

Shah, A. M. 1988. "The rural-urban networks in India." *South Asia: Journal of South Asian Studies* 11(2): 1–27.

Staples, J. (ed.) and W. Creek. 2007. *Livelihoods at the margins: surviving the city.* California: Left Coast Press.

Steinbrink, M. 2009. *Leben zwischen Land und Stadt : Migration, Translokalität und Verwundbarkeit in Südafrika.* Wiesbaden: Verl. für Sozialwissenschaften.

Thieme, S. 2006. *Social Networks and Migration. Far West Nepalese Labour Migrants in Delhi.* Münster: LIT Verlag.

Venkatesan, S. 2010. "Learning to weave; weaving to learn ... what?" *Journal of the Royal Anthropological Institute* 16(special issue): 158–175.

Vidyarthi, V. 1985. "Renewable Energy Development Alternatives: Village Experiences and Indicators for Policy." *Economic and Political Weekly* 20(45/47): 1953–1960.